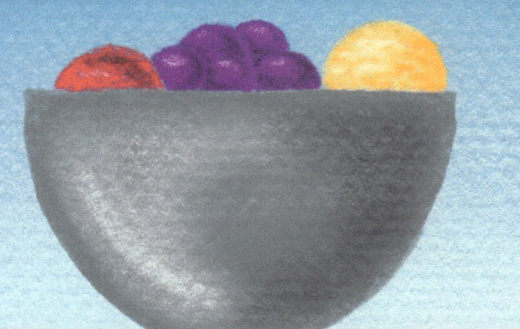
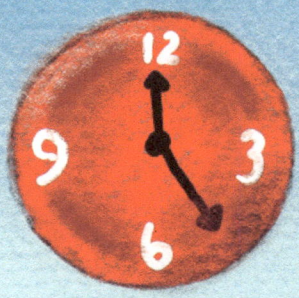

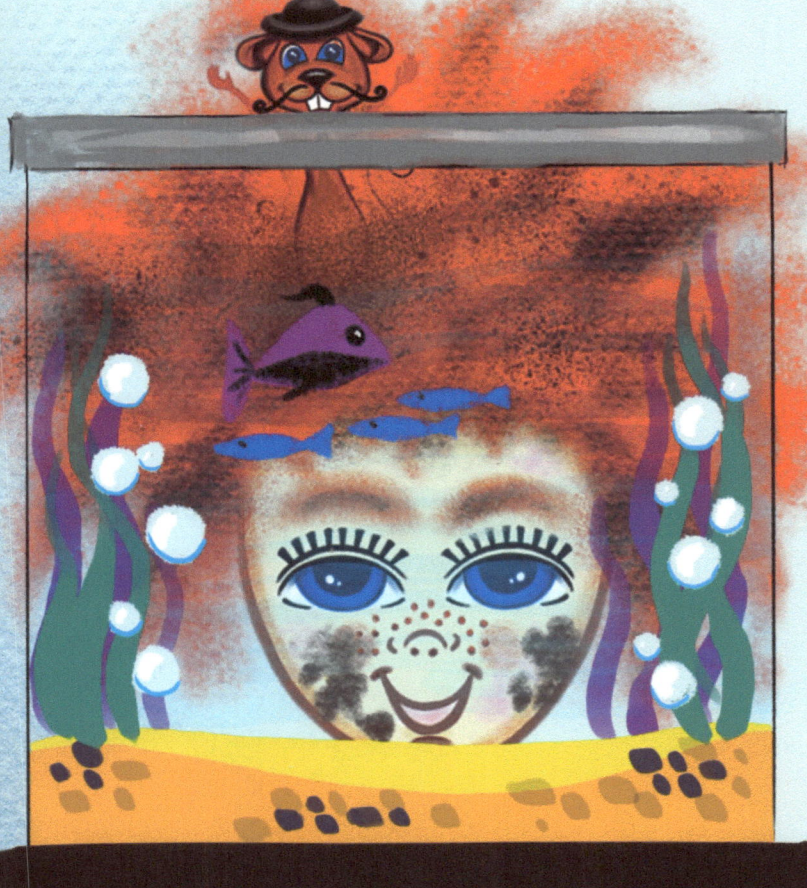

Rebecca Pecca
time to play.
Where do you
want to go today?

I like creatures
swimming free.
Then to the ocean,
it will be.

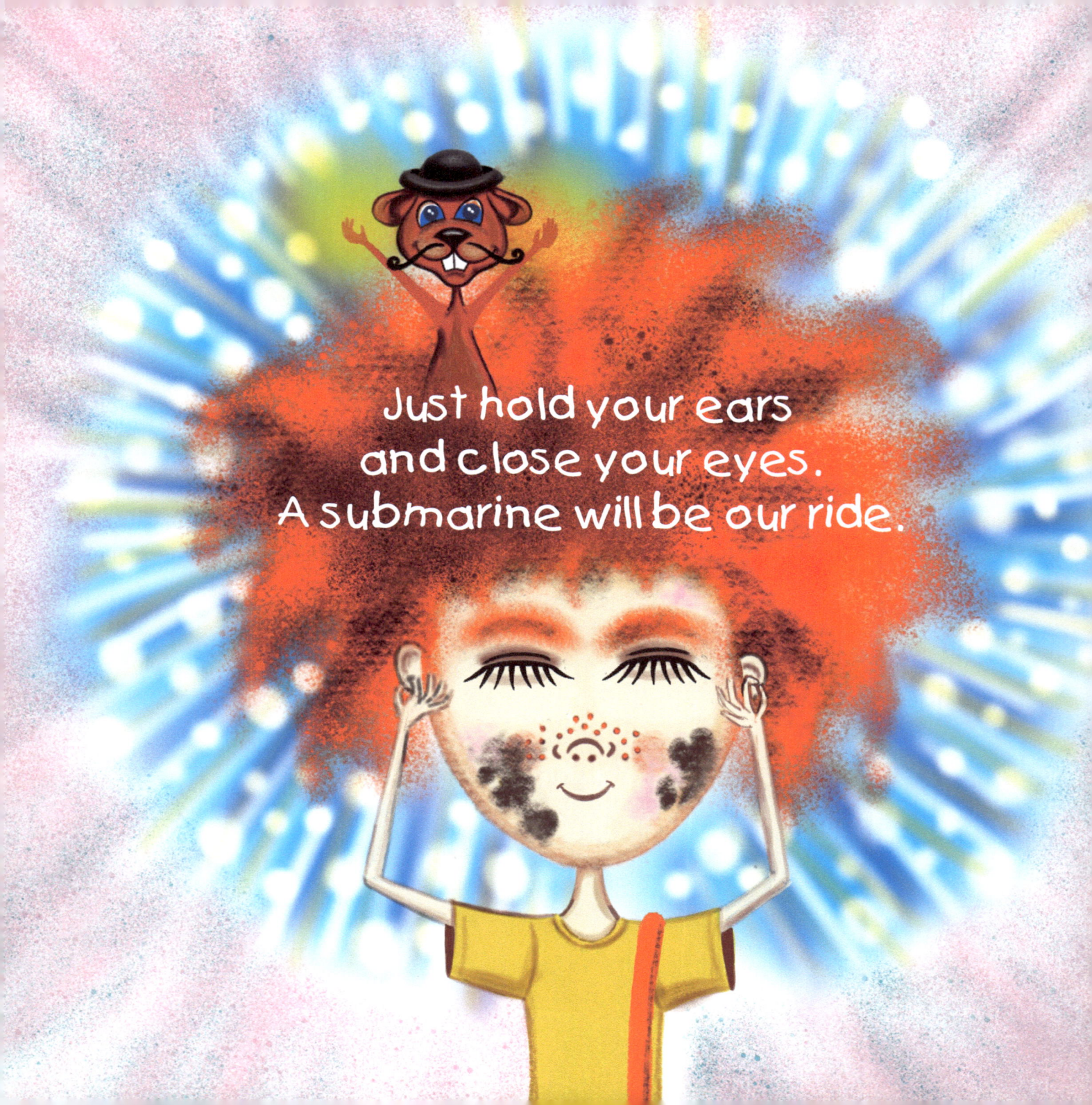

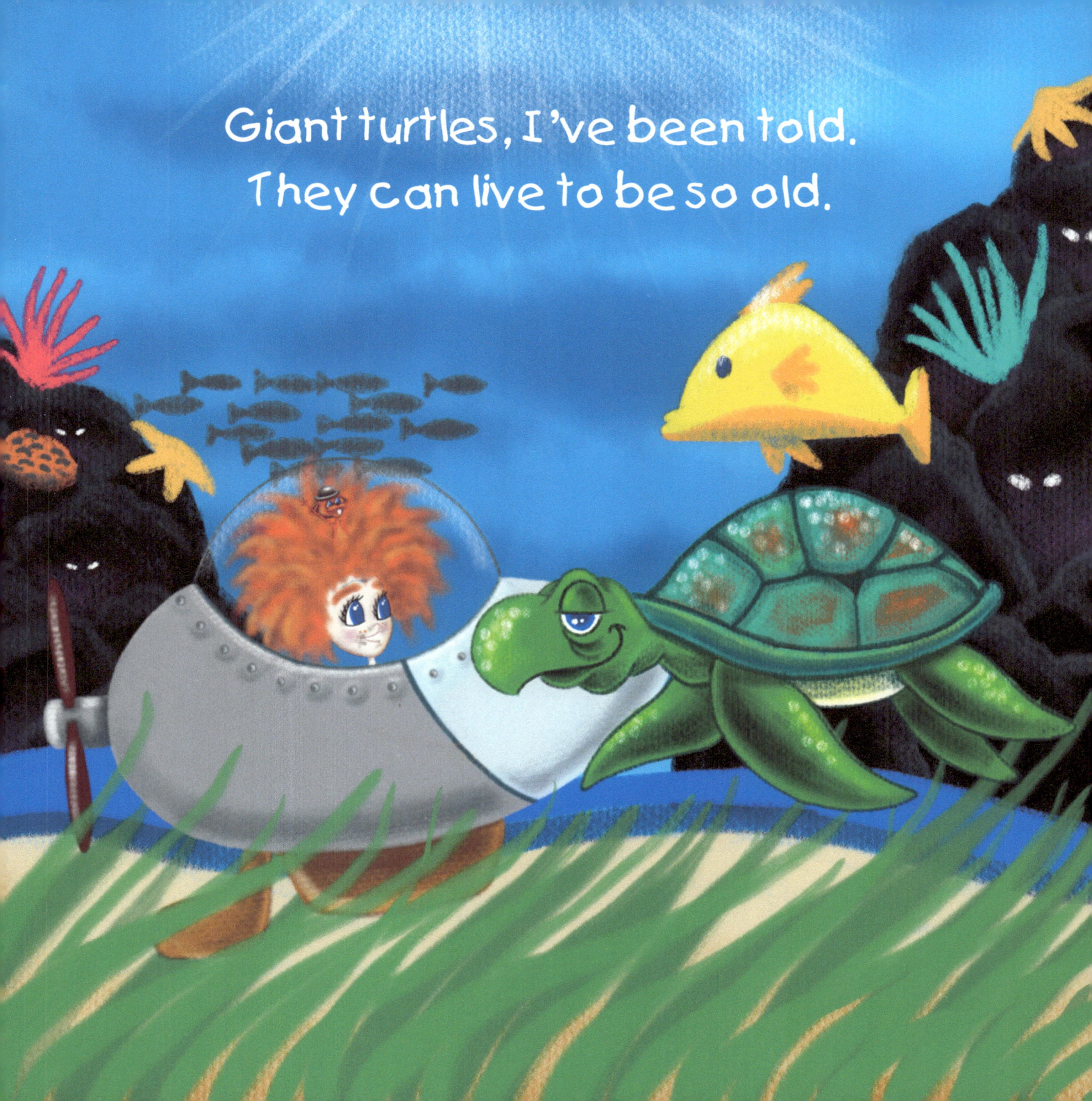

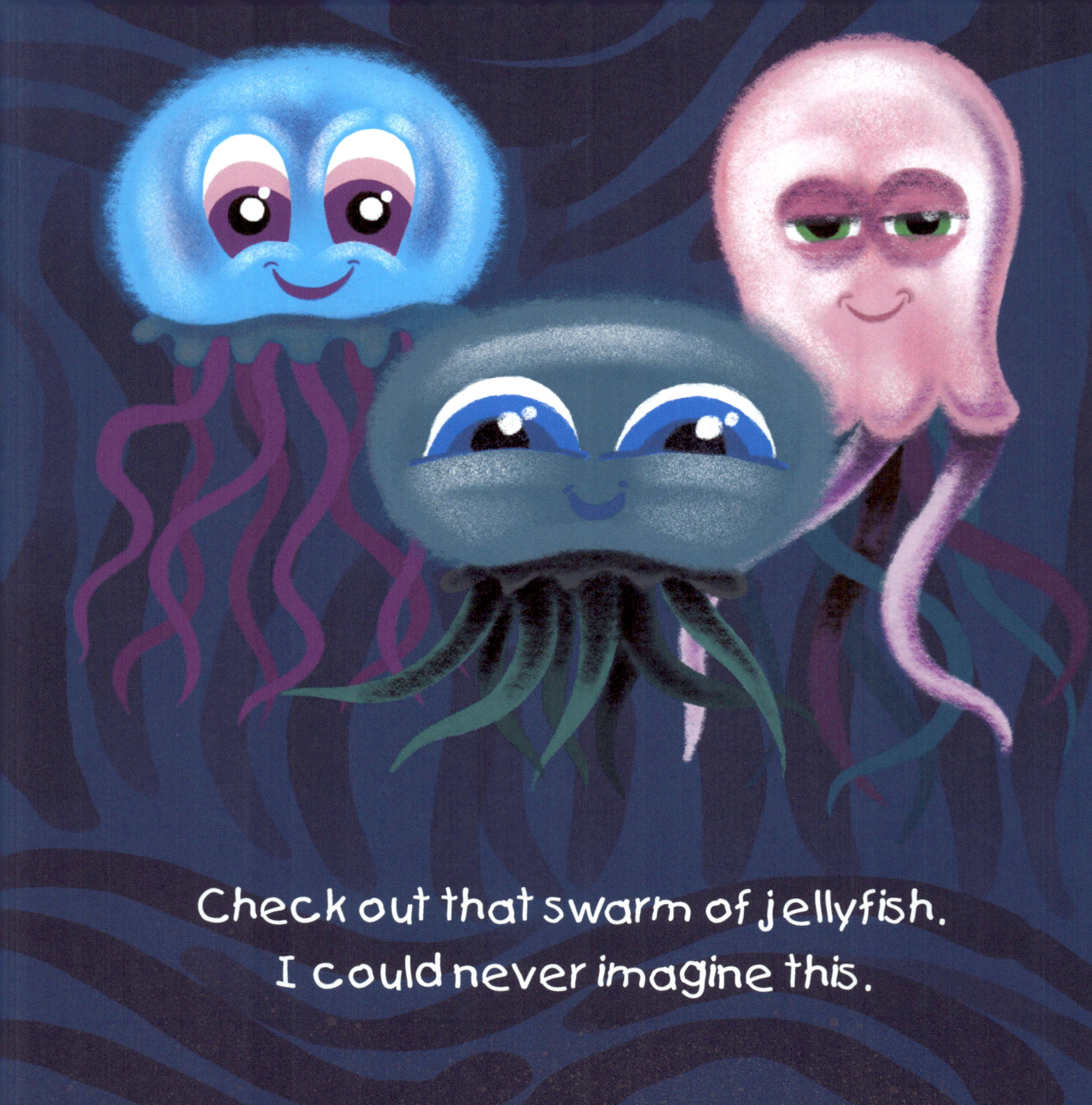
Check out that swarm of jellyfish. I could never imagine this.

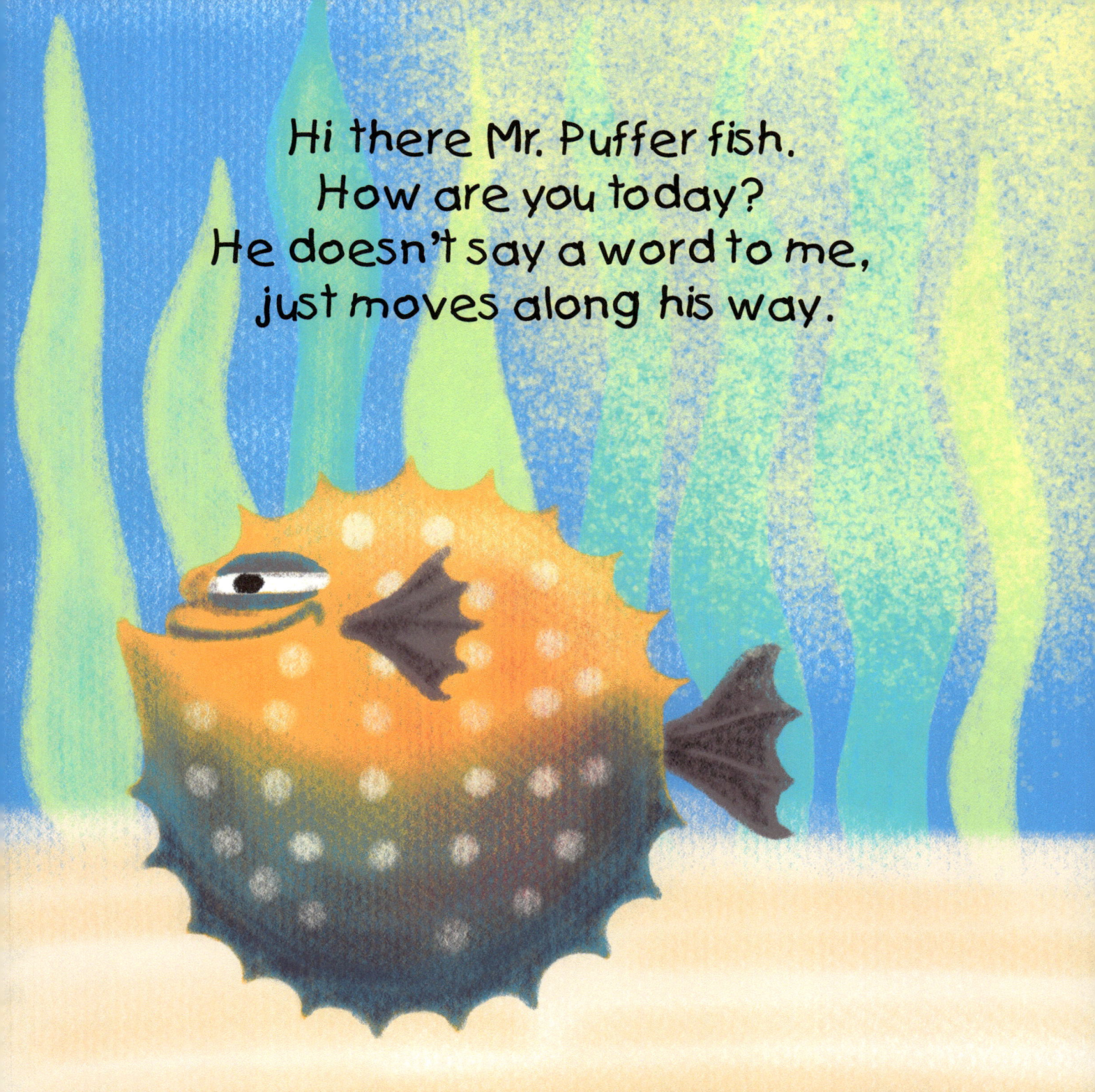

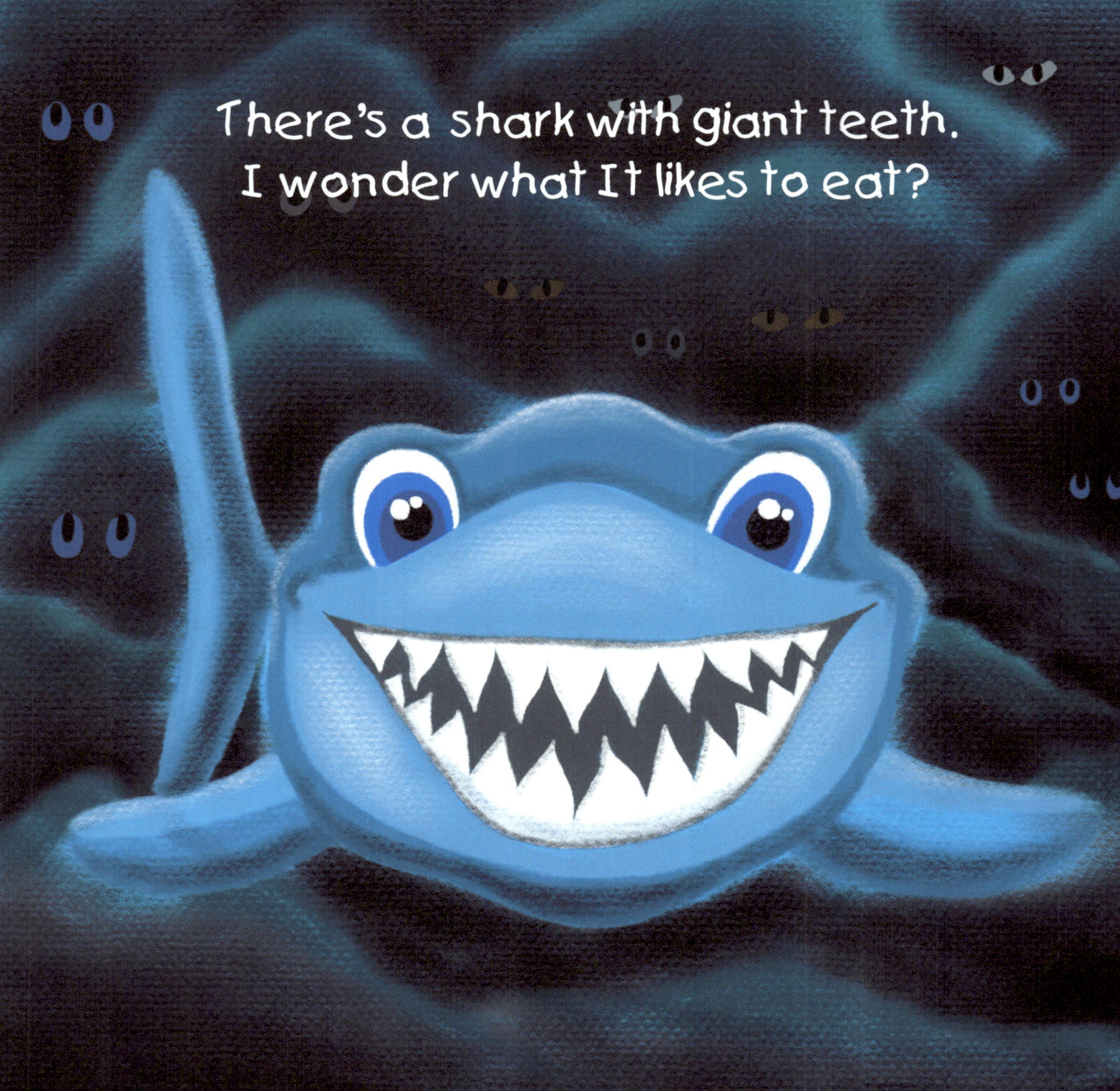

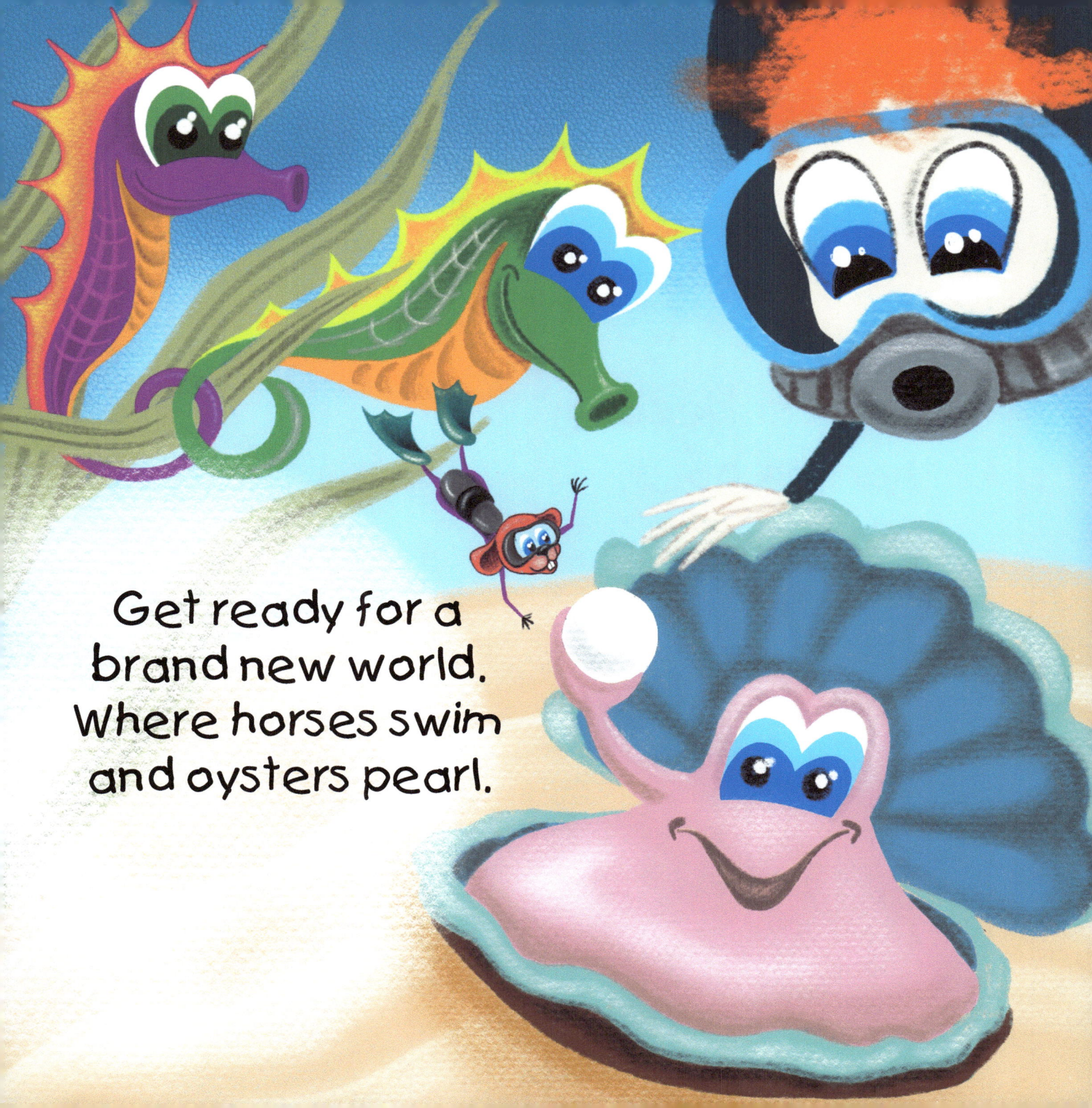

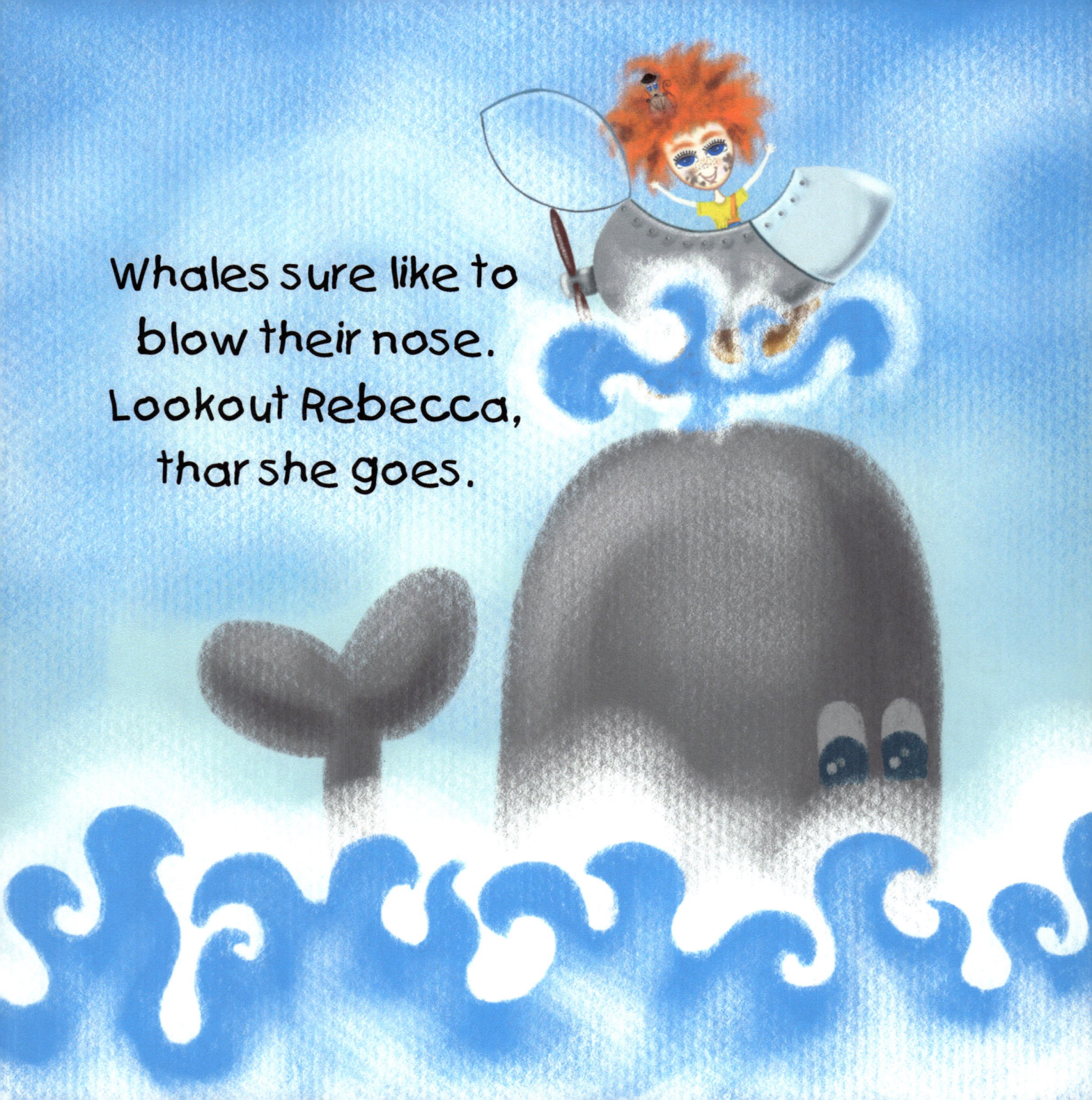

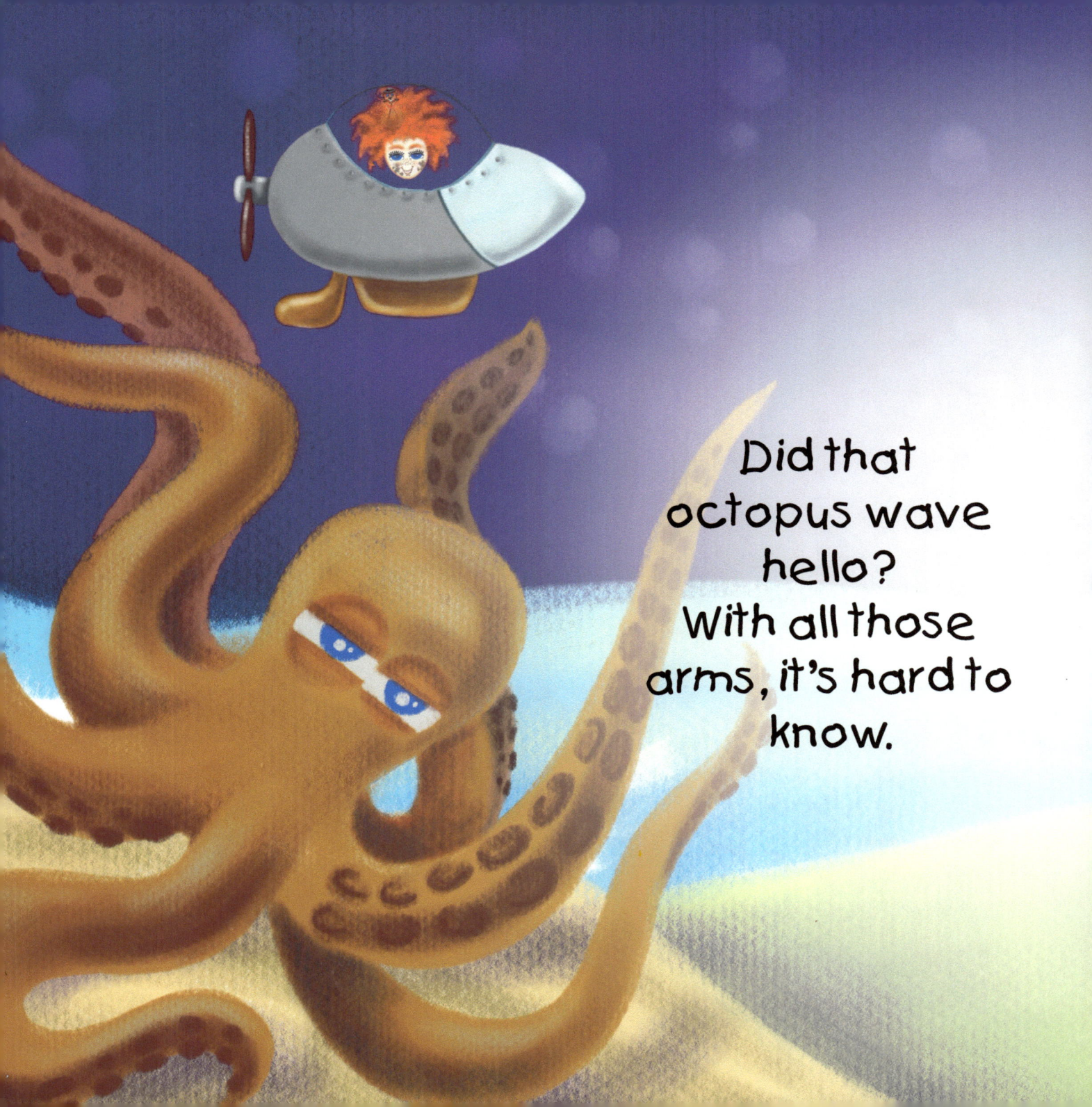

Did that octopus wave hello? With all those arms, it's hard to know.

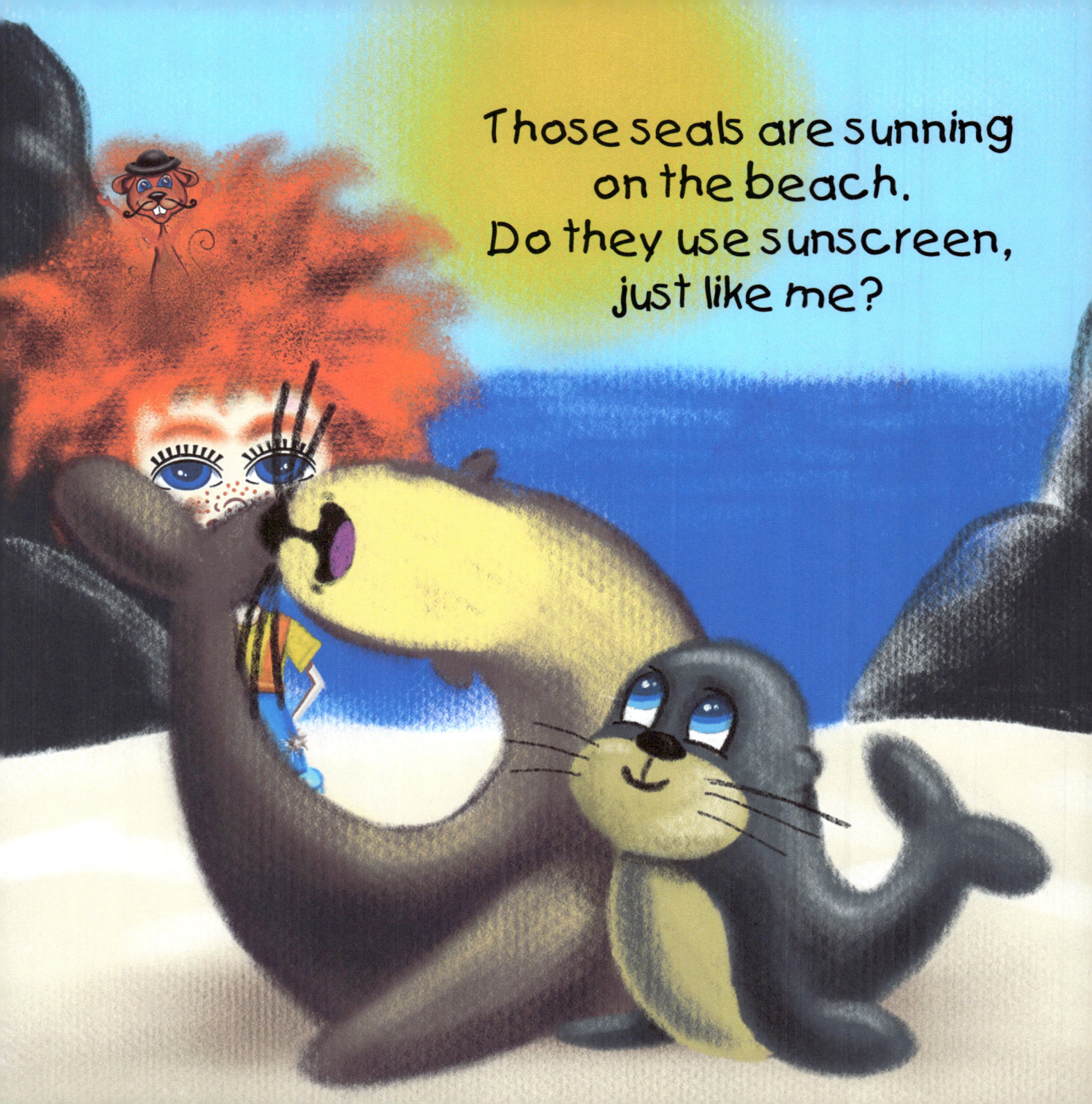

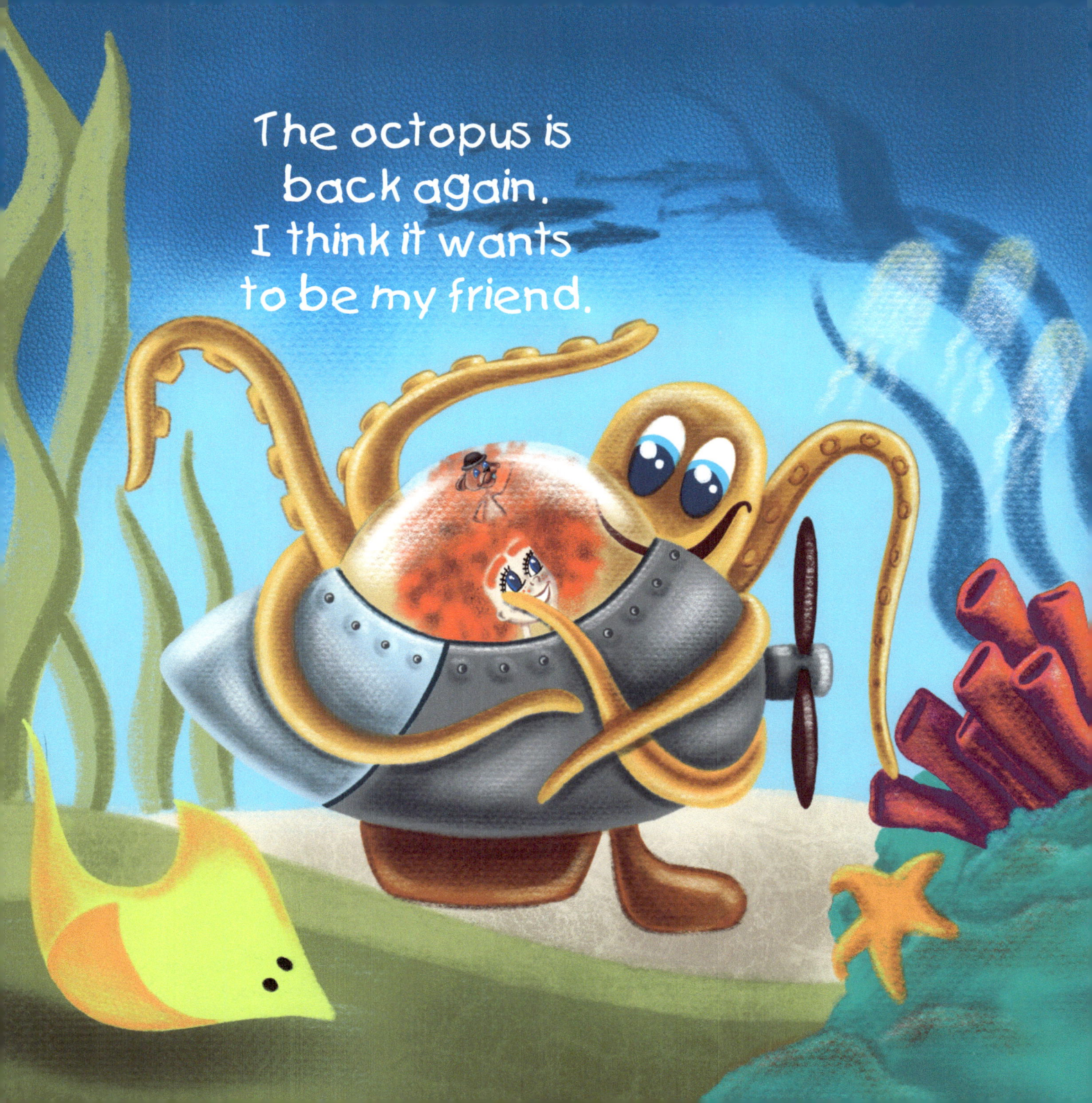

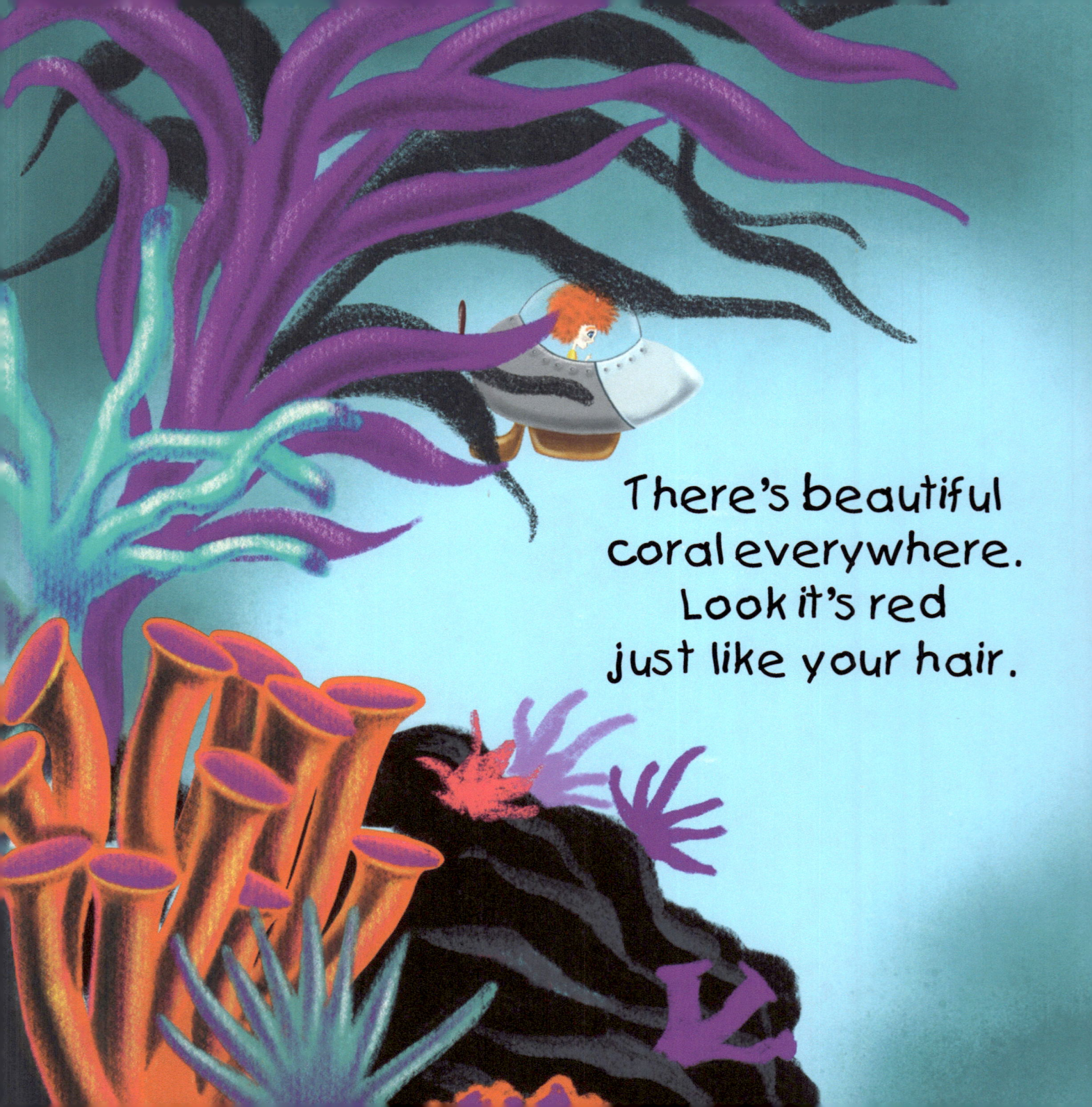
There's beautiful coral everywhere. Look it's red just like your hair.

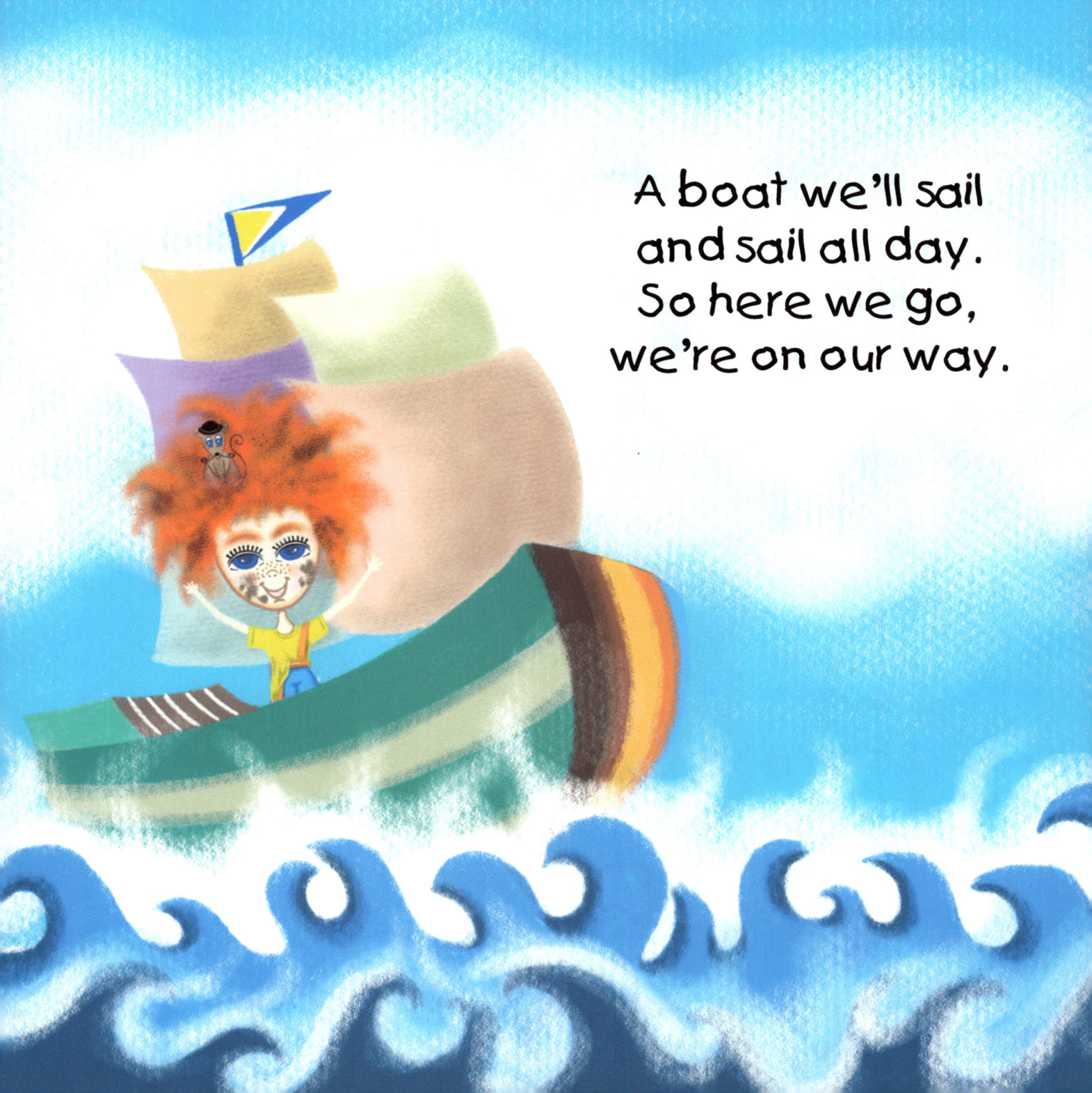

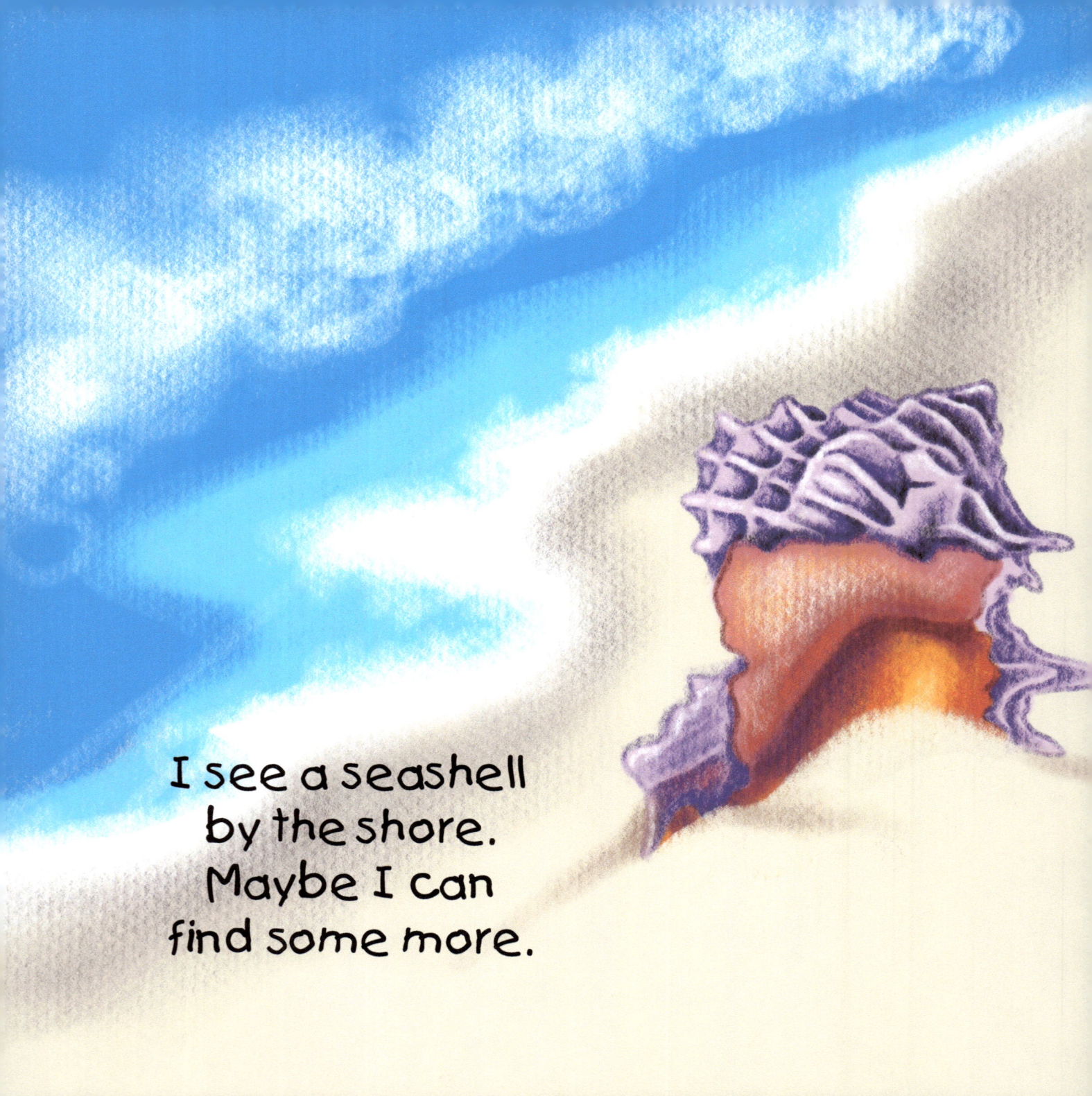

I see a seashell by the shore. Maybe I can find some more.

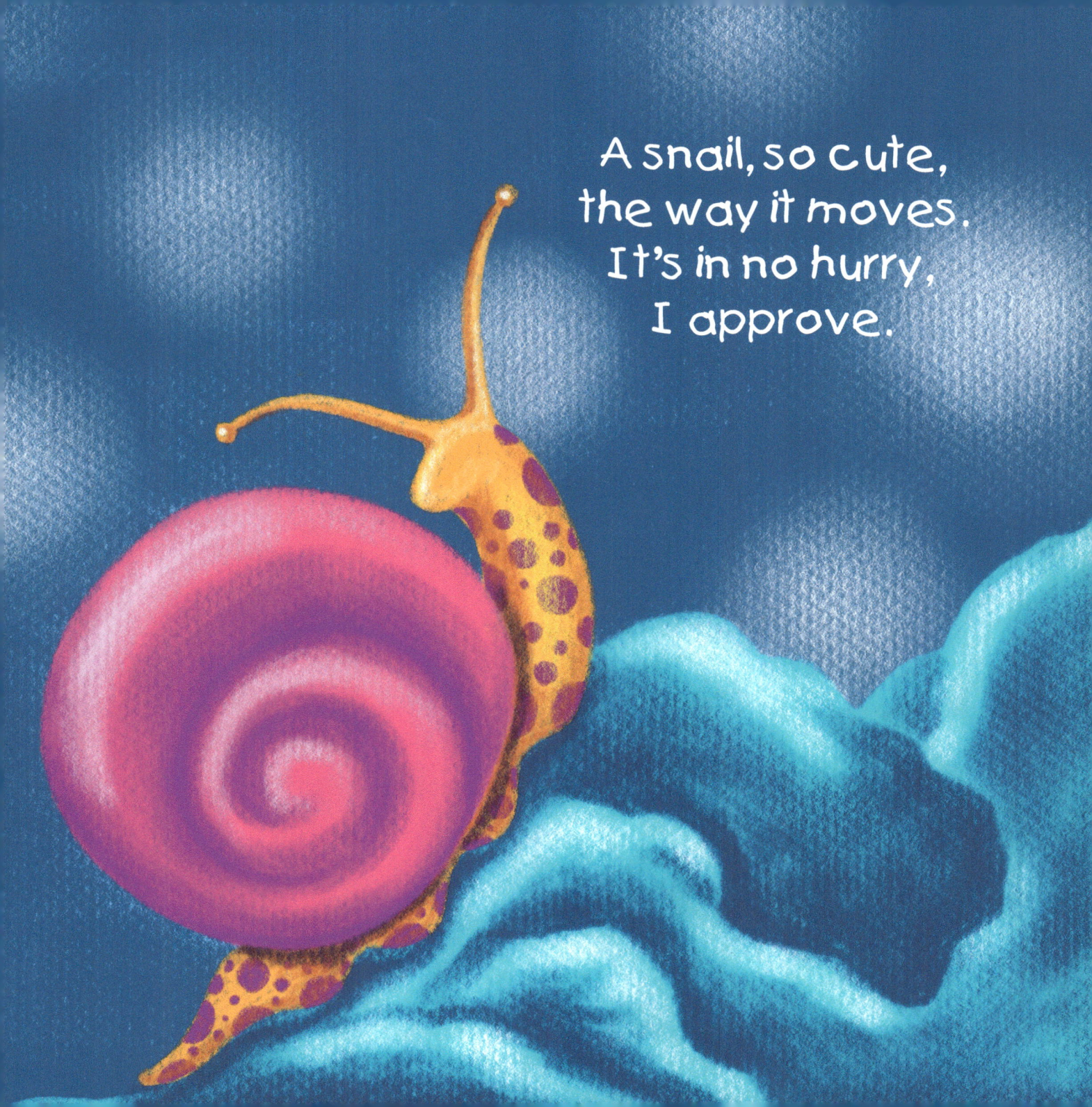

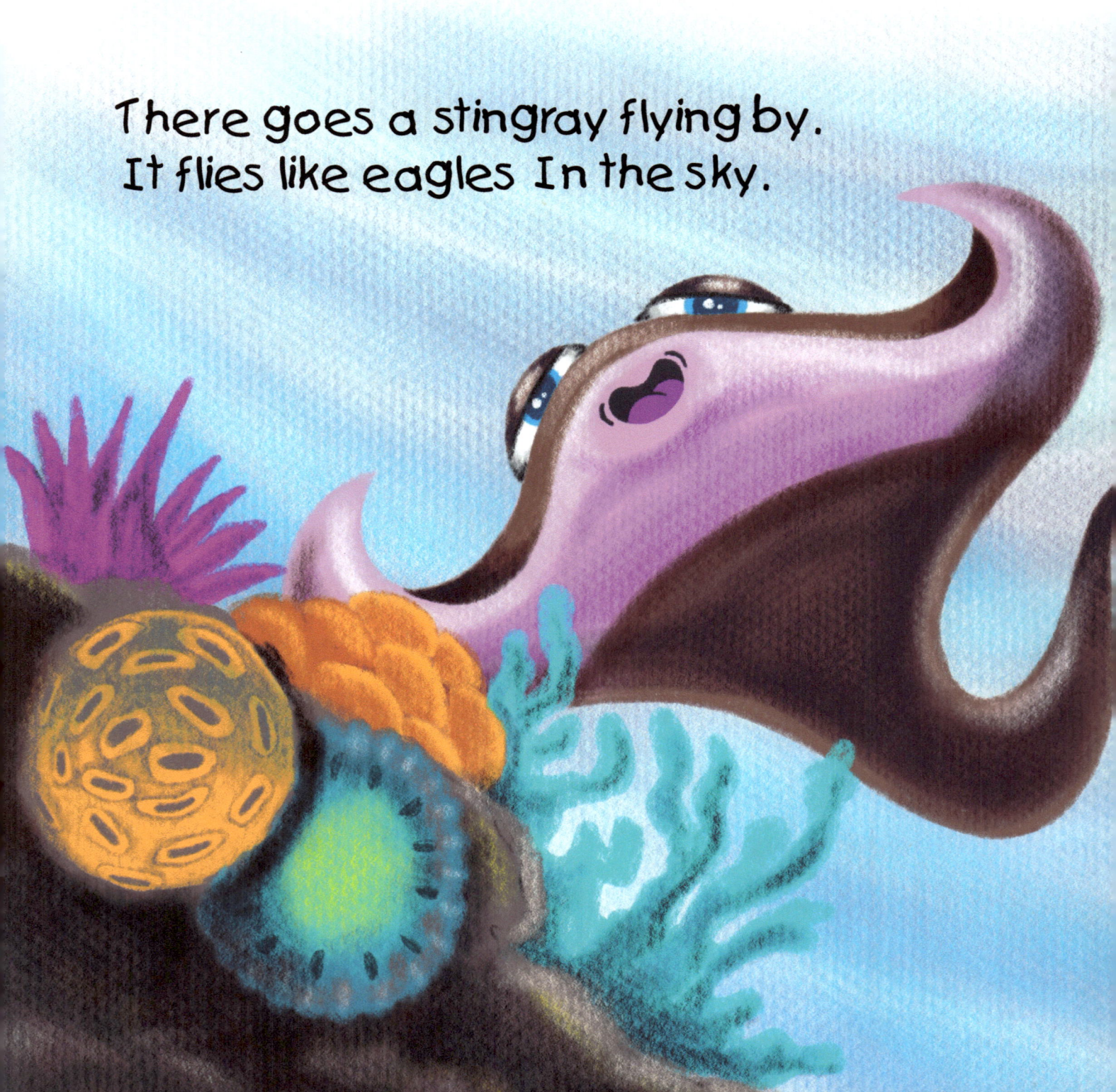
There goes a stingray flying by.
It flies like eagles In the sky.

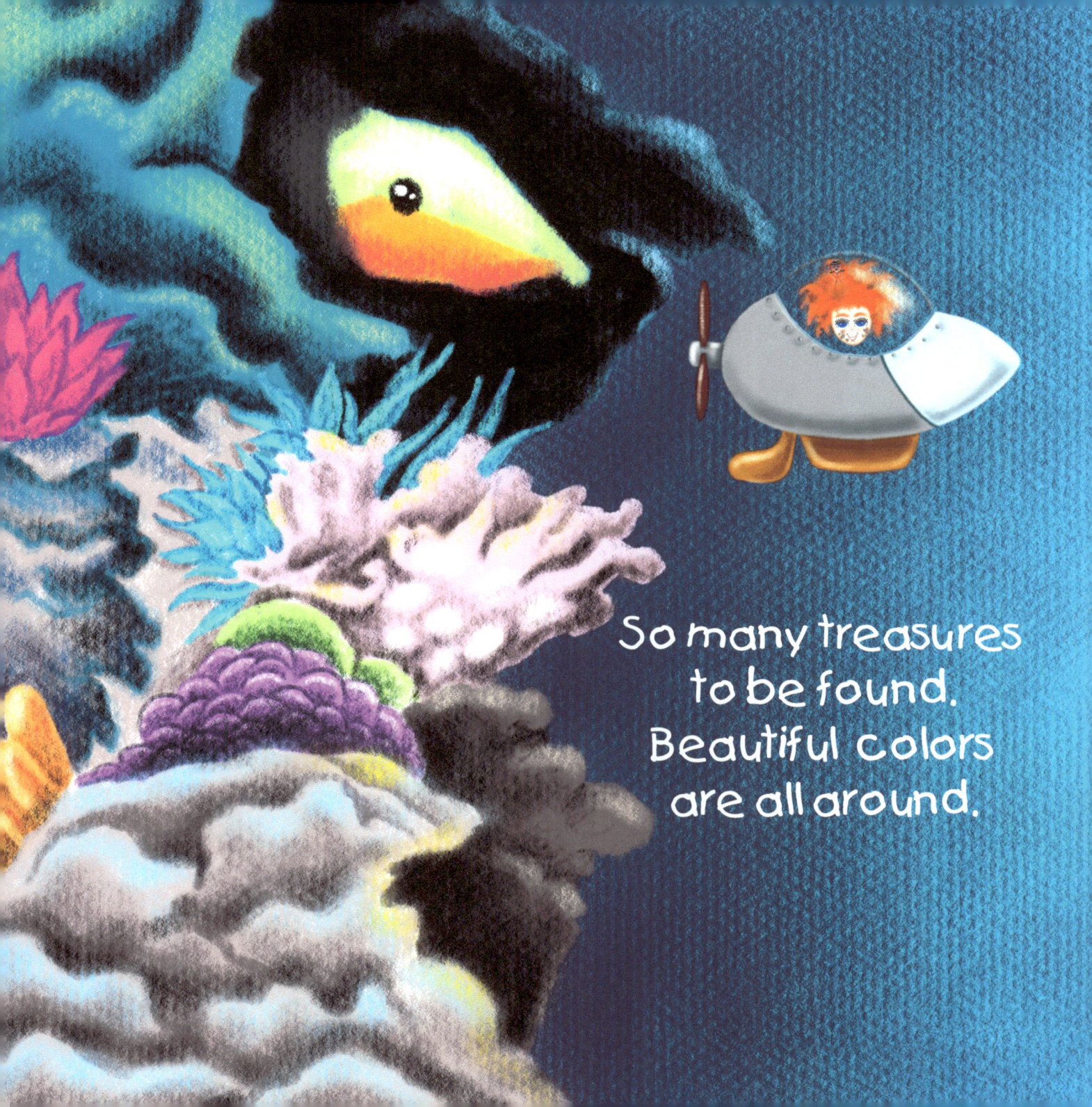
So many treasures to be found. Beautiful colors are all around.

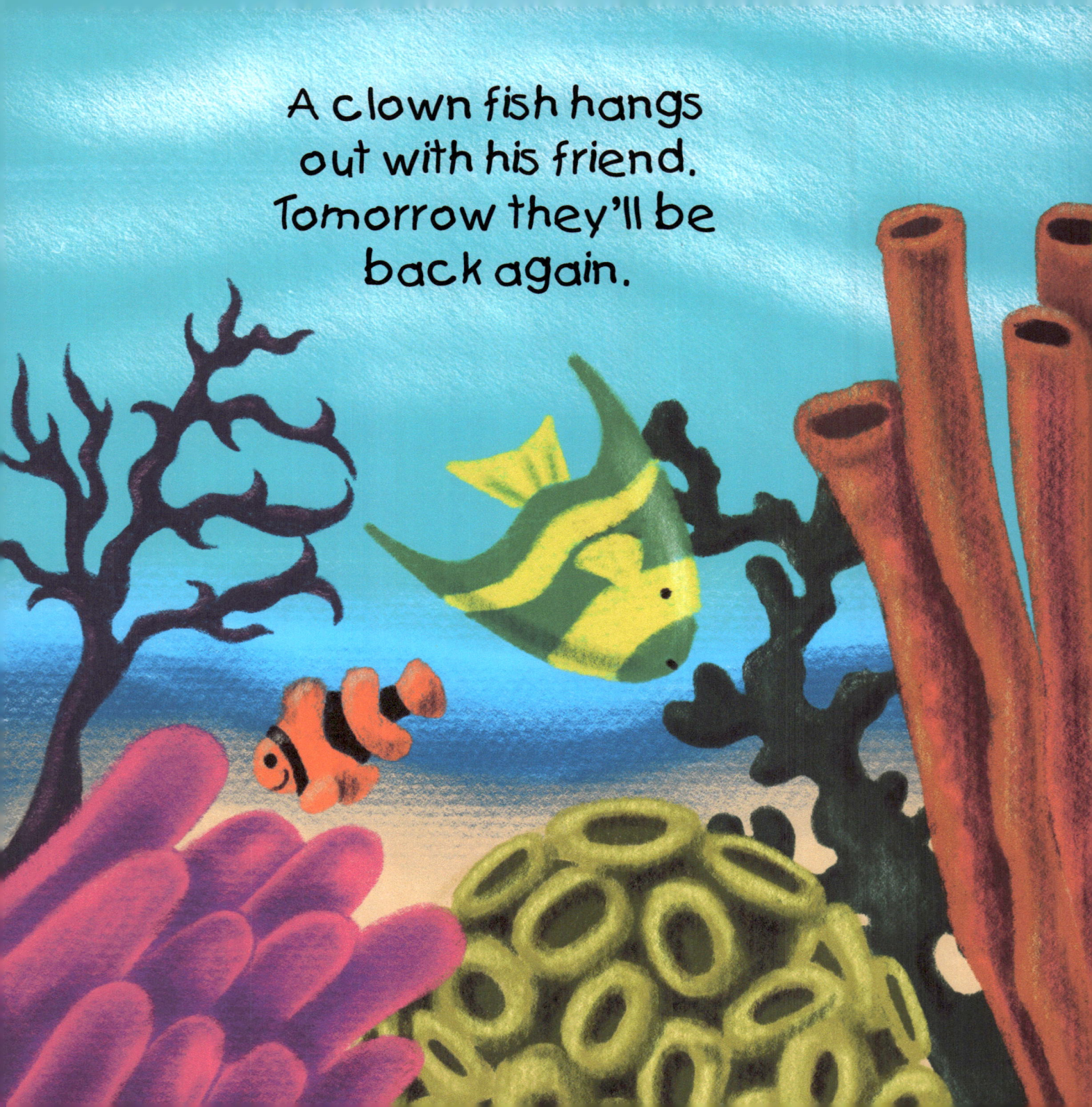
A clown fish hangs out with his friend. Tomorrow they'll be back again.

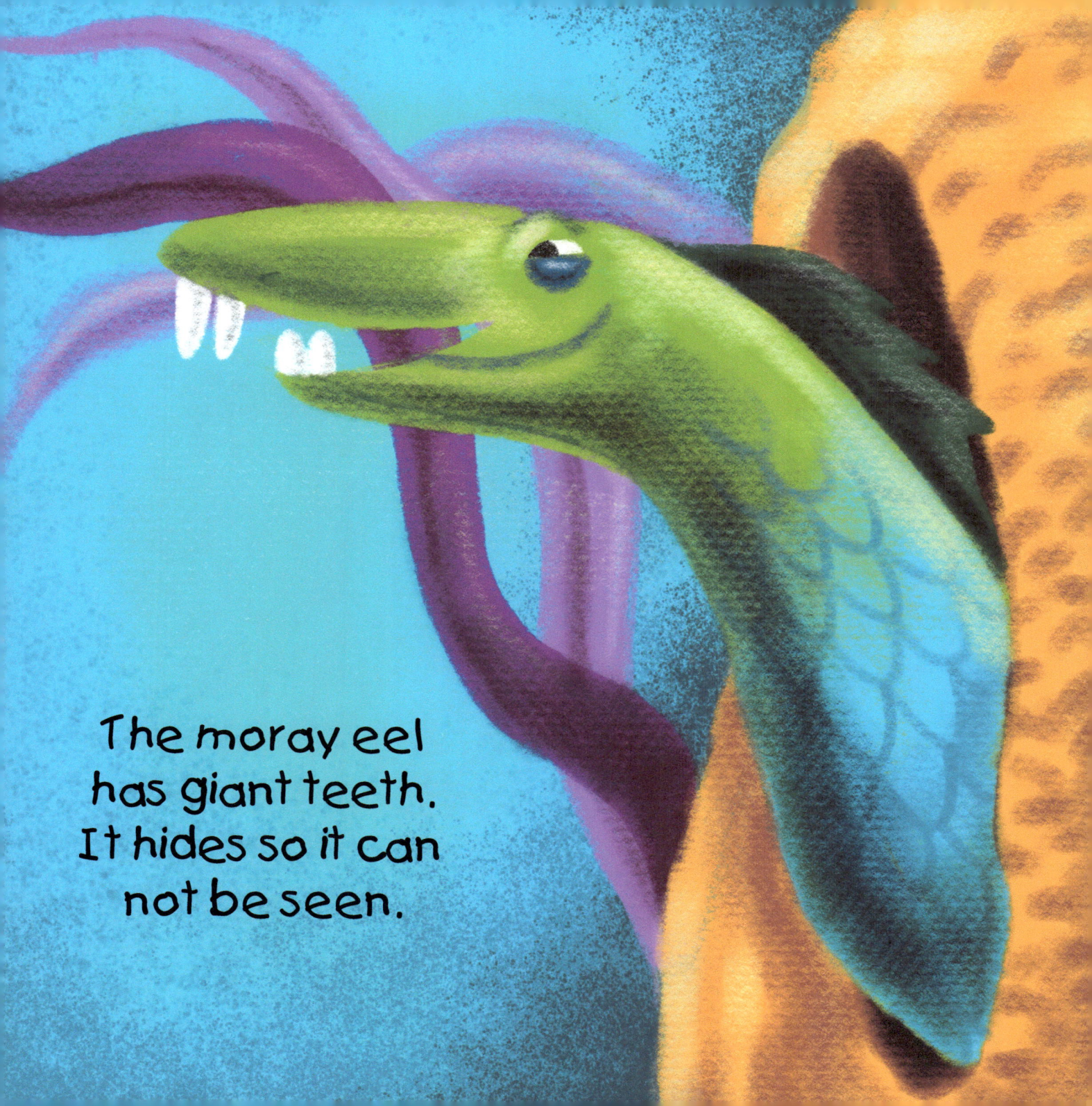

The moray eel has giant teeth. It hides so it can not be seen.

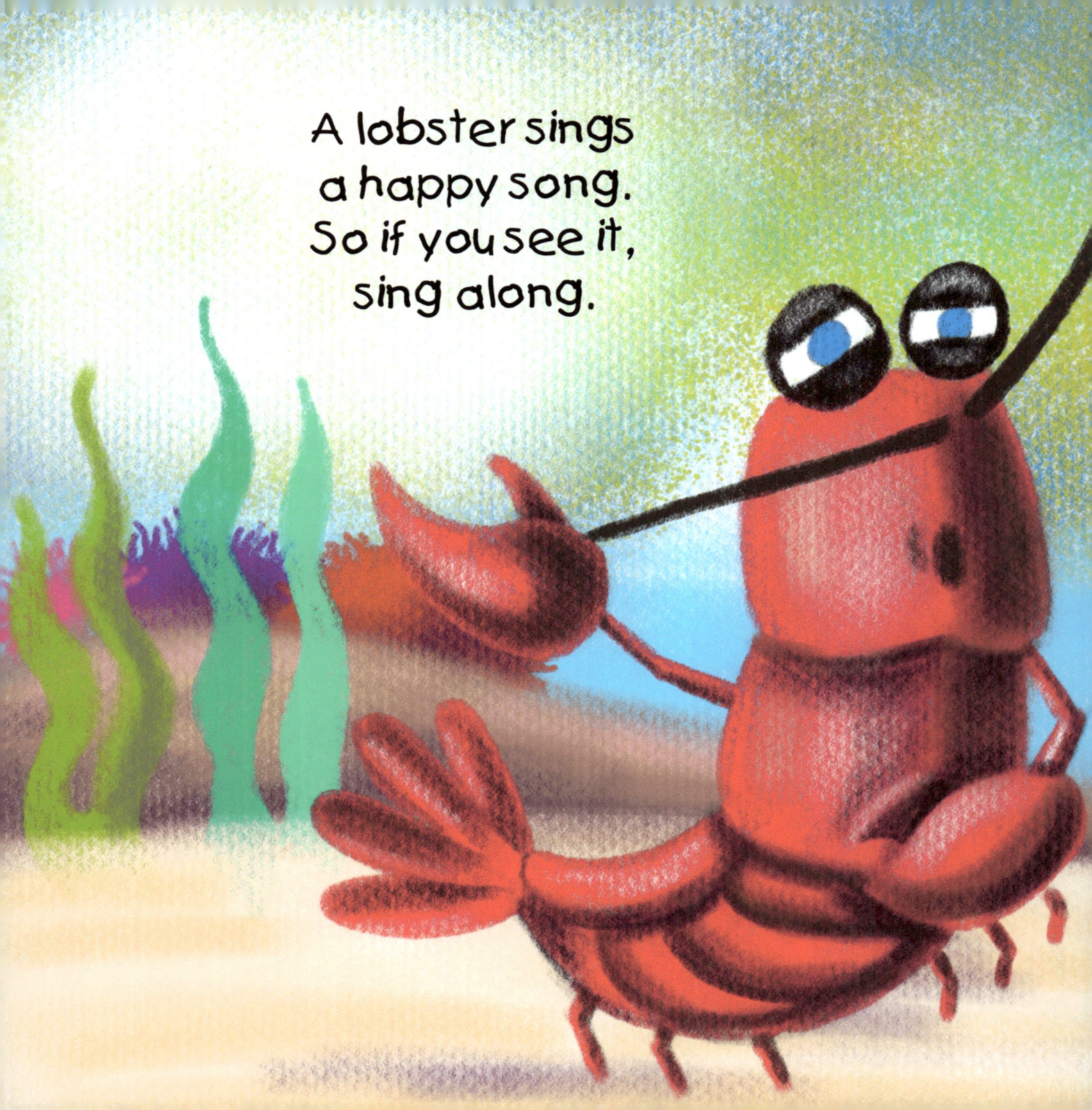

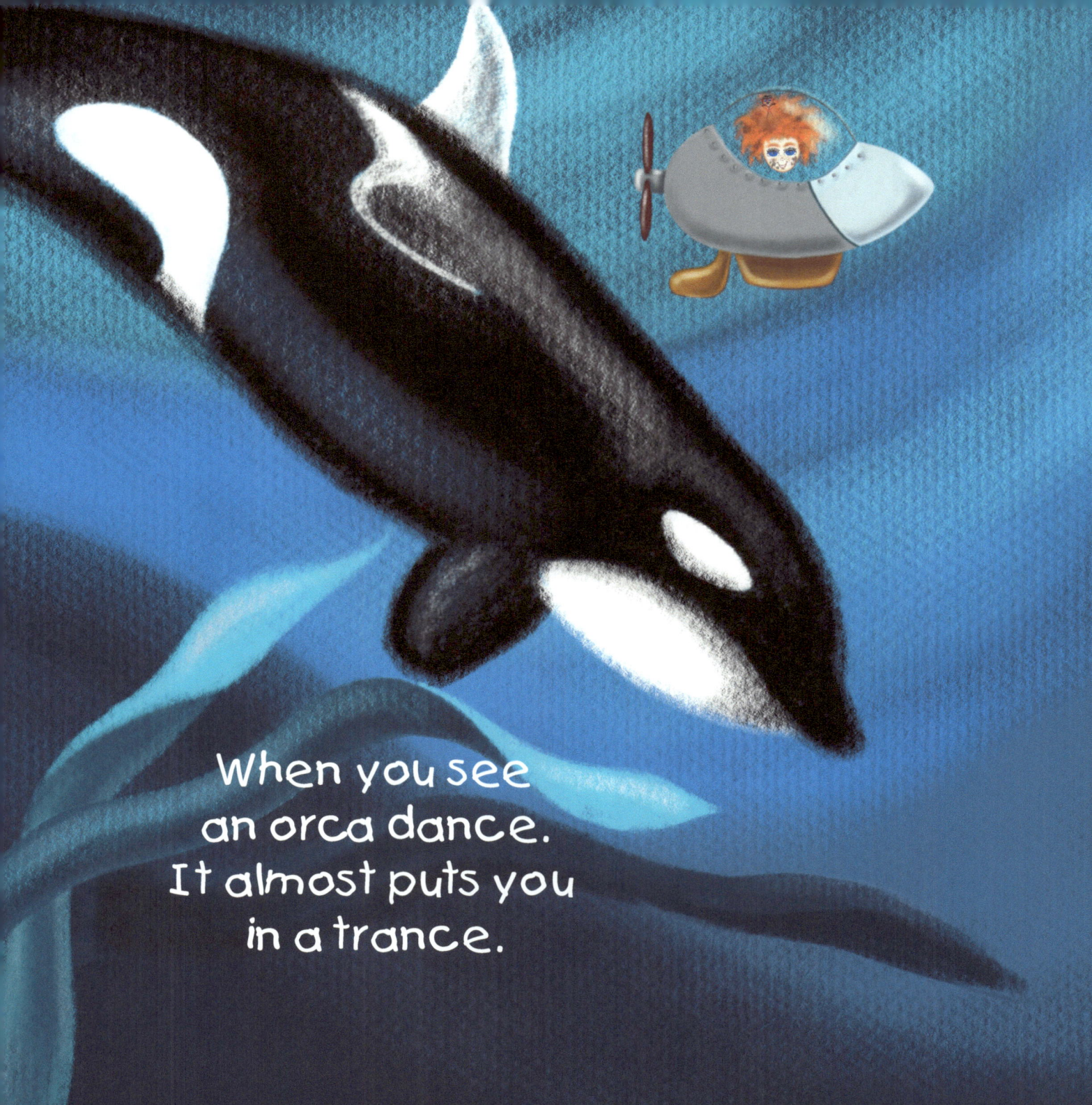

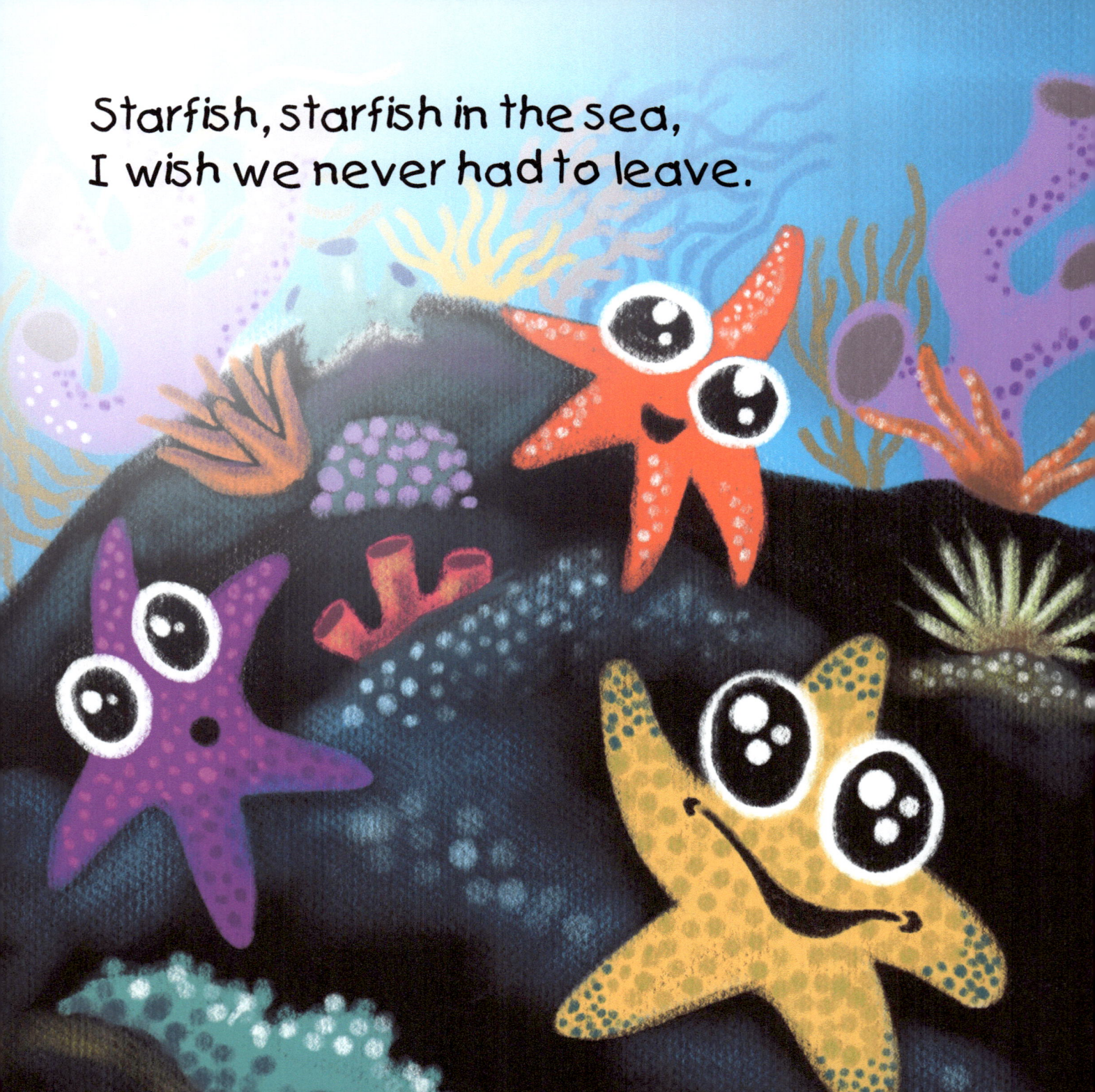
Starfish, starfish in the sea,
I wish we never had to leave.

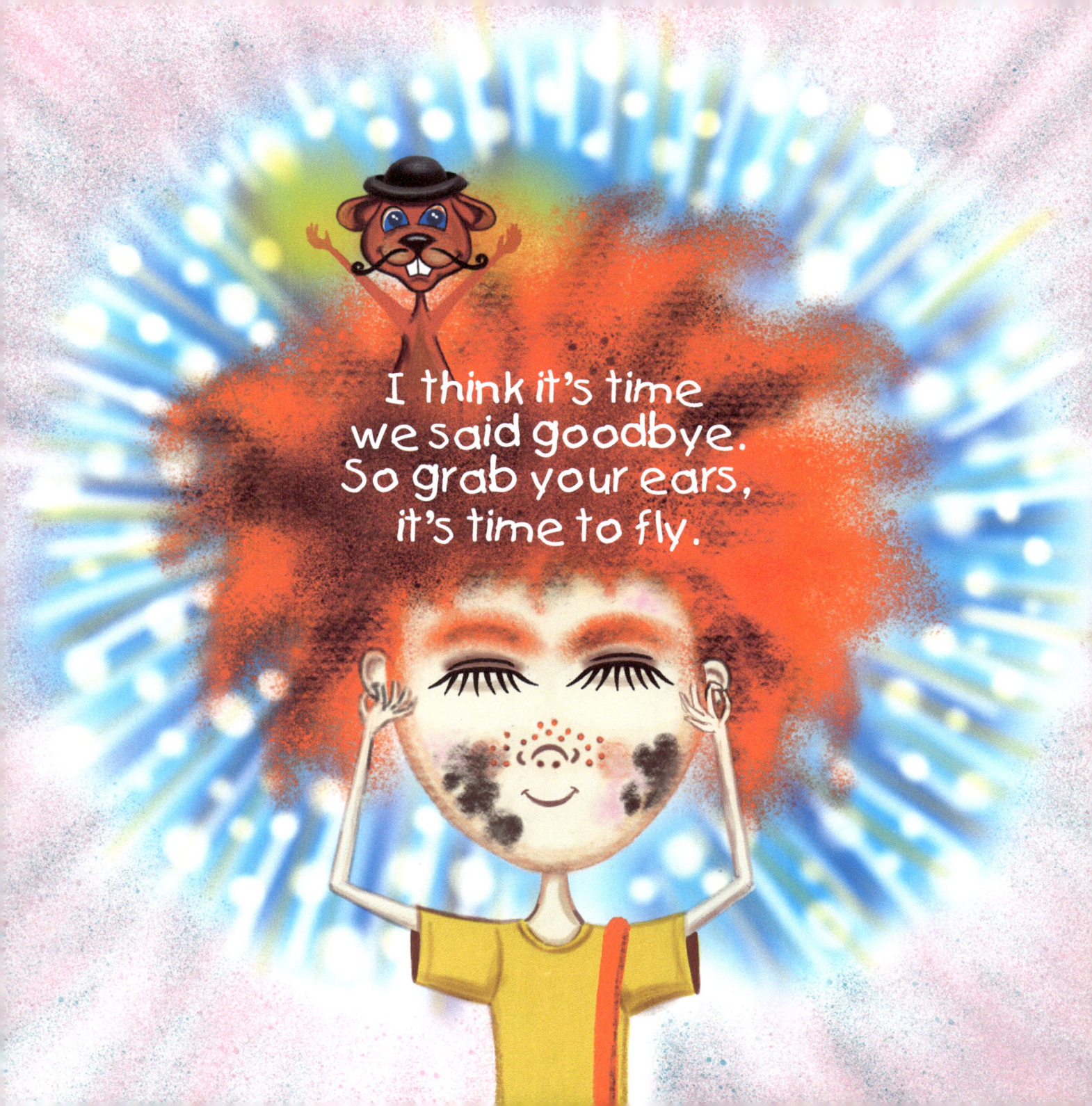

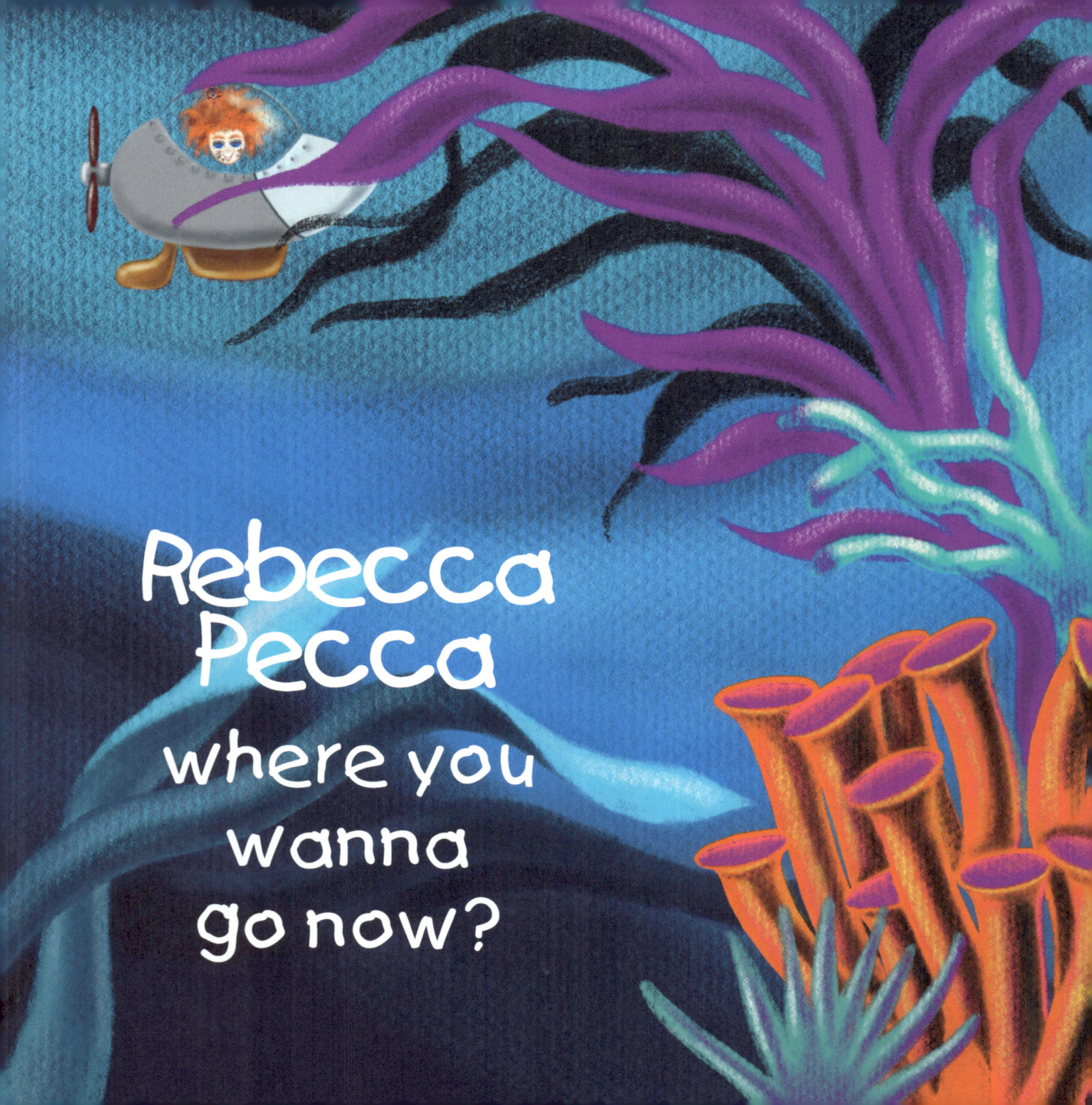